Stock Market Investing 1x1: The Complete Wealth Creation Guide

How to generate sustainable cash flows and invest in highly profitable assets incl. Stocks, ETFs and Real Estate

Andrew P. Hammond

ISBN – 9798597301587

Table of Contents

An Introduction to the World of Stocks

What do you think of when you think of the term' stock market investor'?

Do you think of Wall Street and the high-flying, adrenaline full suited men and women who dart around from computer to telephone in a frenzy, trying to make as much money as possible before the markets close? Perhaps you're envisioning a scene from the blockbuster movie The Wolf of Wall Street.

If you know your history, you may be aware that the first stock markets actually existed centuries ago. Evidence suggests that countries like France had similar systems to the current stock market as far back as the 1100s, although these systems were nowhere near as important or as impactful on the world like today's stock markets are.

As we know them today, stock markets are not a modern concept but instead started to form around the 1500s. Again, these systems didn't affect the world as today's stock markets do, but how they worked and their reasons for existing were reasonably similar.

To fund businesses, to grow the economy, and to generate wealth.

There is a very long and very complicated explanation of why stock markets exist and their impact, but there is a ton of information on this subject online you can read any time. However, for context, I'm going to give you the TL: DR version.

Let's say you have an idea to start a business selling coffee mugs. You have a deep feeling that you've got the best idea, and you're going to reinvent the coffee mug into something revolutionary. However, to get started, you're going to need money, known as capital. You need to make the mugs and develop your product. You need to market and spread awareness, and you need to pay your staff and so on.

In short, you need to spend money to make money, money that you probably don't have to begin with. This is where the stock market comes in. Anybody can buy stocks, and shares, in your company for a price that typically depends on how much your business is worth. Just to keep the numbers simple, let's say your business is already worth $100,000.

You may need more money upfront, so you sell 40% of your business and turn this portion of your business into stocks you can sell. You break the 40% down into 100,000 shares. Quick maths, the stock portion of your business is worth $40,000, broken down into 100,000 shares means each stock is worth $0.4. Very affordable.

Your business goes public, and you sell every single share. You now have $40,000 to spend on your business. You can make all your coffee mugs and market everything, and over the value of your business skyrockets to a tasty $1,000,000. Since your business is worth 10x more, the value of your stocks has jumped to $4. The value of the stock portion of your business is now worth $400,000.

The people who initially invested in your business sell their shares back to you, and you can do the same thing all over again, continuously making and growing money. At least, that's the idea. As a buyer of stock, you've invested in a company, the company has used your money to grow, and now you make money on their profits. This is precisely what we're focusing on throughout this book.

Have you ever wanted to be financially secure? Have you ever wanted to make some money on the side of your full-time job? Does money stress you out, and unexpected bills that arise throw you and your plans back for months, maybe even years at a time? Don't worry; you're not alone.

While risky and not guaranteed to make money, there is no doubt that there is money to be made on the stock market as long as you put your mind in gear, get educated, and are proactive in making the very best decisions possible.

This book aims to guide you through absolutely everything you need to know when it comes to getting started buying and selling on the stock market. We're going to be detailing what you need to be focusing on, what kind of mindset you need, and even exploring some of the key strategies to help you make money.

It doesn't matter if you're trying to get rich, want to grow your savings accounts, or simply want enough money to go on another vacation once a year without it having to affect your bank balance too much, there's something within the following chapters for everyone.

This is a book for beginners with everything you will need to know to get you started. If you've already begun trading or you're just starting with the basics, you may already know a lot of what's written in this book, but you may find some more beneficial chapters towards the end regarding strategies and techniques.

I know how hard and overwhelming it can feel to start out facing the stock market world from personal experience. Everything seems so confusing and massive, so I'm writing this book to break down the basics, share some clarity on the different elements involved in stock trading, and to boost your confidence when it comes to finding your way.

And with that, we're ready to begin, and we're going to start with the most important aspect of becoming a stock trader: your mindset. Let's get into it.

Chapter One:

The Mindset of an Investor

First things first, if your mind isn't in the right place to make sound, grounded decisions, stock market investment is not suitable for you. I'm not saying this to put you off because anybody can learn and train themselves to have a sound and grounded state of mind, but this is something you're going to want to work towards before you even think about making your first trade.

Stock market investing can be stressful and emotional at the best of times, both positively and negatively. Going back to the coffee shop example, and perhaps an example I'll use throughout this book, just for simplicity, if you x10 your investment, of course, you're going to be over the moon. However, if you're caught up in your success and think to yourself;

"Wow, I'm amazing! Look at this amazing stock I picked and how much money I made," and then proceed to invest everything you have into that same stock without thinking, and then the stock losses value, you're going to be worse off than you started and for no reason whatsoever.

On the other side of the coin, if you invest a lot of money into one stock and it starts to lose value rapidly, you could freak out and panic, literally watching the value line dropping and dropping as you see your wealth seemingly disappear. Watching this happen can be devastating and incredibly stressful, but if you're making decisions in this state of mind, are they going to be the right ones?

Probably not.

As a stock trader, you can't let emotions dictate your actions and choices, and this is a great lesson that you can apply to the rest of your life. Not to sound like a self-help book, but say you're falling out with your partner. If you talk reasonably and calmly with them, even if they themselves are flying off the handle, this is far more productive than both of you just mindlessly shouting at each other. The same logic applies to stock market investment.

So, you need to be calm to be a stock investor? What else? While you can apply and train yourself to have the perfect state of mind over time, here are some of the traits you're going to want to think about developing, also known as 'The Trader's Mindset.'

Detach from Emotion

As I said above, stock trading can be incredibly emotional if you allow it to happen. There are guaranteed to be both good and bad times during your personal trading journey, and you just have to accept that as the reality of the situation. However, with great risks comes great reward, so if you're able to tame yourself and your emotions, you can have them work for you, rather than create problems in your life.

When I say to 'detach' from your emotions, I don't mean that you should push them down and ignore them forever. What I'm saying is that you don't want them to control you. Let's say, for example, you're in a bar with friends after work on a Friday, and you're excited to start the weekend. You get that first drink in, and you turn around to walk to your table, and someone walks into you on their way past.

They give you a fleeting apology and start to walk away. The drink has gone all over you and the floor. What do you do? Well, naturally, the first thing you might feel is anger. Maybe you want to hit the guy or get him to apologize more? Perhaps you want him to buy you another drink? Perhaps you're full of disappointment because you were really looking forward to the drink and now, you're just feeling sad.

You could lash out and beat the guy up, or you could let it go? Whatever happens, the moment the drink gets spilled, you're going to feel an emotion. It could be anger or sadness or whatever. Still, it's up to you to run with that emotion and let it take you over, aka, going crazy and start making a scene, or you become mindful of that emotion and say to yourself, "okay, I feel this way right now, so how am I going to deal with it?"

This is essential for becoming a successful stock trader. You're going to feel incredibly happy and on top of the world at times, and you're going to be angry if something doesn't go your way. The trick is to notice, acknowledge, and then still be able to make grounded decisions.

Being Present

Being present goes hand in hand with the trait above because if you're not present when you're trading nor focused on what you're doing, you're not going to catch your emotions as they arise. What's more, you won't be focused on making the right decisions.

Let's say you're watching a stock going up and up, and you're waiting for the right moment to buy or sell.

However, your mind keeps wandering off to all the other items on your to-do list, or you're worried about your partner or how you're going to afford to get your car fixed.

These are all valid things to be worried about and things that will need sorting out and require some degree of thought, but you need to start training your mind to realize there's both a time and a place for this kind of thinking to happen. The time you spend working on your stock career is not the right time.

There are plenty of ways you can retrain your focus and become present, such as journaling, mindfulness meditation, and so on. Find what works for you and get your brain into the moment. Get it working for you right here, right now.

The Ability and Willingness to Learn

The very best and most successful traders know one key thing, and that's that they don't know everything. There's always a new strategy or skill to learn. There's always more information to take on board. Most importantly, there are going to be lessons throughout your career disguised as mistakes.

You will make mistakes, and you will mess up. You'll do something wrong or make a wrong decision. This could have a big or small outcome. It doesn't matter. What matters is your ability to reflect on what you've done, analyze it, and then work onwards from here.

As an investor, you need to make sure you're dedicating time to the end of each and every day where you look back at what you did, highlighting what you did great and what elements you can improve upon. Should you have made a trade earlier or later? Why did you make the decisions you did, when you did?

Were you emotional? Should have taken a break instead of continuing to trade? Could you have better software with different features? Do you need to learn how to use your existing software better? Do you need to understand more about your stocks before trading? Whatever elements of your trading experiences you look at, you need to drop your ego and realize there's always room for improvements.

You just need to be willing to do so. I find that it's best to keep a journal or diary on hand where you can write down and reflect on your experiences at the end of every day, giving you a clear insight to look back on to find ways to improve.

Remember You are Human

Every human being on this planet makes mistakes. Nobody is perfect. Every human needs to look after themselves, i.e., eating the right diet, getting exercise, and getting enough sleep to ensure they function correctly. You are included in this bracket.

Sure, a strategy could be to sit in front of your computer for 18 hours a day trading and hoping to hit big. After all, the more time you're in the market, the fewer opportunities you'll miss, right? Wrong. A crucial part of being a trader is making sure you're doing everything in your power to give yourself the best opportunities, and this means being able to look after yourself and be as close to peak performance as possible.

Sure, there are going to be days where something happens, and you can't shake yourself out of this mindset. Perhaps you'll get physically ill or injured. That's just life. However, it's how you deal with these situations that will determine your success. Do you have the mentality when you're ill to take the day off to recover, or, in your unsound state of mind, are you going to start trading $ 10,000's worth of trades?

Being Decisive

In the trading world, the amount of time you hesitate to decide is an indicator of how confident you are in your own abilities and how you see yourself. If you're sure you want to make a trade for a lot of money and you're ready to do, and then something, a niggly feeling inside, stops you, why has this happened?

Sure, there's always going to be an element of doubt in everything you do but doubting yourself and hesitating could be the make-or-break seconds that tip the scale of whether a trade is successful or not. The stock world moves too fast for you not to be confident in what you're doing.

As I said before, you are almost guaranteed to both make money and lose money when you're trading. As we'll repeatedly explore throughout this book, the key thing to remember is that trading is not about investing in one stock and suddenly making millions in one overnight trade. That only happens occasionally, and if you have millions to invest in the first place.

The vast majority of traders make money with small yet consistent wins. They maximize their small wins, perhaps 1 or 2% here and there, and minimizes their losses. Maximized wins and minimized losses mean profit over time, not all in one go over no time at all.

Decisiveness is the key to making this happen.

Capable of Taking Risks

As with anything in life, you need to be able to take risks. Yes, there is always a chance that you invest $10,000 into a company and it goes bankrupt, and you lose everything. Of course, this is a very dramatic situation and one that the chances of happening are scarce, but I'm not saying it to scare you. I'm saying it because it's not a 0% chance it won't happen.

As a stock trader, you're opening the door to risk with everything you do, but without being able to take those risks, you're not going to succeed. Of course, you're going to do everything you can to minimize your risk factor and make reliable decisions, as we'll explore later when we discuss how to get educated and actually choose which stocks you're going to buy, but be aware that it's all a risk.

This is all a matter of perspective. If you ask someone on a date, you're taking the risk of looking stupid and being rejected, but if you don't take the risk, you never even have the original chance of going on a date. The same logic applies here, so if you're not already much of a risk-taker type, then it's time to start thinking about molding your mindset.

Take Responsibility

There's a common belief out there among some traders that 'the market is out to get them' or 'it's not in their favor and is screwing them over.' I can't help but laugh as I write this, but I'm sure you've heard similar things outside the trading world. They may find something like 'oh, the whole world is again.' me.'

It isn't. The stock market doesn't conspire to make you lose money. It's inanimate and doesn't care whether you win or lose. It just exists, just like the rest of your life. The world and universe aren't out to give you a bad time. Your perspective is just telling you it is because you're afraid of taking responsibility and ownership of your own actions.

When it comes to stock trading, what you make or lose is a direct consequence of the actions you've made, and you'll never be able to grow and improve as a trader until you accept this and, coupled with the points above, are then able to learn from your mistakes.

Your actions are always your own. Own them.

Enjoying Yourself

Finally, and perhaps most importantly, you have to learn to enjoy yourself. If you're not enjoying your trading experiences, you're not going to be doing it for very long, you'll resent the time you spend investing, and you'll have wasted so much time learning all about the process.

Trading, while it can be serious, can be very exhilarating and very rewarding. Even when you're serious, such as spending a day completely locked into a day of trades, this can be enjoyable in itself, like try hard to win in a video game.

While taking it seriously, make sure you appreciate your journey as you go, relishing in the things you're doing, such as making your first trade (which we'll be covering in a bit), creating new accounts, setting up your workspace, setting your target investment milestones and goals, and so on.

Like all things in life, the process of learning something new and becoming successful at it, even if you're only focusing on small wins, is super enjoyable and rewarding, so ensure you're giving yourself the time and the space to do this.

So, to give you the lowdown and a kind of takeaway for this chapter, over the coming weeks, I want you to think about how you can;

- Recognize and detach from your emotions

- Become more present

- Develop the willingness to learn from experiences

- Remember, you're an imperfect human being

- Becoming more confident in your choices and decisions

- Take responsibility for your actions

- Enjoy what you do

Developing all these traits will come in time, but I start with this chapter because it means you can get started right away. While working on these, let's start focusing on the actual art of trading itself and how to get set up and ready to go.

Chapter Two:

Setting Yourself Up

For the purposes of this book, I'm going to assume that you're going to be trading at home, be that on a PC, tablet, or phone, or ideally a combination of all three, but you may be wondering how you actually get set up and ready to go. What do you need, and how your station needs to be set up for success?

This is what we're going to diving into within this chapter.

First things first, you're going to need a dedicated trading space. Some people may have an office at home, the corner of a living room, or somewhere like this. If you can convert your garage or spare room, this could be ideal. The point is that you need a space where you can go into said space, and your mind will go, 'I'm in trading mode now.'

The key considerations you'll want here is making sure your space is quiet, and you're going to be free from distractions. You don't want pets, partners, or kids running around you when you're trying to concentrate, nor do you want background television play or distractions from outside. Of course, the chances are you won't have access to the perfect place, but you'll want to get as close to perfect as possible.

I'll also say I don't recommend setting up an office area in your bedroom. It can be convenient and easy, but having your workspace in your bedroom just doesn't work. Your mind will be torn between sleep mode and work mode all the time, and this can make you restless and stressed.

So, assuming you know of a space, you need to get yourself a desk and a chair, preferably optimized and ergonomic because you're going to be spending many hours here. I highly recommend getting yourself a standing desk that can be switched between sitting and standing and a chair with lumbar support. This will make sure you stay fit and healthy instead of destroying your posture by sitting in a chair all day.

Next, you need a computer. Ideally, a powerful computer with at least 8GB of RAM is recommended because you're going to be running multiple applications, and this needs to be backed by a fast internet connection since you'll be looking at a ton of information and content in real-time. You're also going to want two monitors (make sure your PC supports this), so you have more virtual space to work with.

If you have a laptop and a PC, a tablet, and a PC, this also works. If you travel a lot, you may want a gaming-style laptop since these will have larger screens and more powerful processors for running multiple applications at once. If you get a laptop, also think about battery life.

Now, it's time to get into the fascinating and exciting bit. Setting up your broker account.

A broker account is an online account that connects you to the stock market. It's the middleman that provides you with a platform for buying and selling stocks and typically will have an online wallet where you can keep your funds. Many brokers offer web-based solutions, so you can simply sign in to your account from any web browser to make transactions or offer more features by allowing you to download and install an application to your computer. I recommend sticking with web-based services until you know what you're doing and have mastered the basics of stock trading.

So, how do you choose a stockbroker?

In this book, strategy-wise, we're going to be focusing mainly on day trading strategies because you'll see a faster return, but even if you're interested in long-term trading, you'll need a broker to handle your deals. You can see the table below to get some ideas on what brokers are out there and what they have to offer.

Stockbroker	Minimum Deposit	Regulated By	Details
Pepperstone	$200	FCA, CMA, DFS, ASIC, and more	Offers spread betting and CFD trading. Offers services for both retail and professional traders. Can trade indices, FX, and more.
eToro	$500 ($50 in the USA)	FCA	Offers a platform for trading stocks and crypto-assets. Allows trading for CFDs.
Plus500	$100	FCA, ASIC, CySec	Voted the UK's number one stock trading platform. Can trade Forex, stocks, Options, Indices, cryptocurrency, and more.
FxPro	$100	FCA, CySec, SCB	Has won multiple awards for their stockbroker services.

Stockbroker	Minimum Deposit	Regulated By	Details
			Can buy and sell in a vast range of global markets.
			Specializes in Forex trading.
Fondex	$0	FSA, CySec	Won multiple awards for their online broker services.
			Low trading costs compared with other platforms
			Specializes in CFD and Forex.

Information and data correct at time of writing – Jan 2021. All data is subject to change at any time, and readers will need to check each platform for the most up-to-date information and prices. This table is for guideline purposes only.

These are just guidelines to what brokers are out there and what you can expect. Ideally, if you're just starting out, I highly recommend starting with a platform like Plus500 because it's very beginner-friendly, has low costs, and gives you access to everything right off the bat.

If you're strapped for cash and want to get started on a small-scale, then a platform like Fondex could be ideal because there's no minimum deposit and low prices and costs. Either way, take a look at some of the brokers out there, many of which offer free trials and sample accounts, so you can see what works best for you.

Of course, when you're starting, you're not going to really know what works best for you, because you need the experience to make up your own mind. This is why it's recommended to try several brokers, perhaps creating your own shortlist with pros and cons and then making a decision in six months or so.

To get a broker, simply head over to their website and create an account. Most accounts are free to get started with (minus the minimum deposit). Ensure you're using a strong password since you're potentially going to have a lot of money in your account and won't want it to get lost or hacked.

Finally, the last thing you want is a journal. This could be a pen-and-paper diary, the Evernote or RazorJournal app, or even just the notes on your phone, although I recommend having a dedicated writing place. This is where you'll put all your notes about each trading session, can track your progress, set yourself goals, and explore new ideas. It's your hub for getting all the information and content out of your mind, so you're free to work.

And with that, we come to the end of this chapter, and we're ready to start your first day of training. Everything is set up, and your mind is hopefully in the right place to become your own investor! Take a moment to congratulate yourself for where you've been and how far you've come, and now get ready.

Now is when you go from zero to hero and actually become a real-life trader and investor on the stock market for the first time.

Chapter Three:
Your First Day of Trading

This chapter will be short and sweet because I know you're excited about getting stuck in and making some money. After I had been reading stock market investment books like this for some time, I remember my first day, had set up my station and was finally ready to make my first trade.

While we're here and before we jump into it, if you're not ready to actually commit real money, let's say you're still saving up or getting your finances in order, then note there are plenty of sample platforms out there where you can trade real-life stocks using fake money, just to see how you would fair.

If you want to build up your confidence in your abilities and see how your decisions now pan out, I highly recommend starting here. Some fantastic services in this area include websites like;

- Thinkorswin

- TradeStation

- Trading 212

- Warrior Trading

- Bear Bull Traders Simulator

Many broker websites and platforms may also offer their own versions, so make sure you look around. If your chosen broker does offer trial services like this, use them because you'll only be giving yourself more experience with your chosen platform and will gain familiarity with how it works.

Now, if you're planning to use real money and make a real investment, this is what you're going to need to do.

Assuming you've set up your broker account and paid in some money, perhaps meeting the minimum deposit, you need to choose a stock to invest in. This can be any stock you want but try to make it affordable and within your budget. At the time of writing, Tesla stock is currently $854.41 a share, and if you only have $500 to spend, you're not even going to get one, and you won't be able to diversify your portfolio. I'll talk about this a bit more in the following chapter, although you can buy part of a share if you really want to.

However, let's say you want to spend $50 on your first stock. Simply search through your broker to see what kind of stocks are currently trending. You're looking for a stock that's either lost value by around 2-3% or one that has risen by about 1%. This is just a fundamental strategy to get started, and we'll cover more complex ones later.

Go through and find a stock you like, looking for a nice stock that looks like it could grow or is growing. If you find one that looks as though it's on the way up, and is starting to rise, go ahead and make an investment.

Now, whichever stock you've chosen, keep an eye on the live graph (this is why you want two monitors, one for the chart and one for your broker), and watch it rise. Keep watching and watching, and when you feel as though the graph is about to stop growing in value, or it does, in fact, start to decrease, then sell the stock once again.

By the time everything has gone through, you may have only made 0.3%. Sometimes you may make 2-3% in a single deal over the course of a few minutes. It depends on the stock, which is where the risk factor comes into play.

However, that's it. You've just made your first stock investment and trade and hopefully made some money on it. I recommend starting with small figures, maybe $10 or $20 here and there so that you can get a feel for timings and how quickly you can react to the market changes and make the buy and sell transactions. When you're ready, and you master your own technique, then you can start scaling up how much you're spending at a time.

As I started writing this chapter, I've had the stock graph for Exxon Mobile open in another tab, a UK-based energy company. Valued at $48 per share, the stock has risen by 1.13% in the last half an hour. If I spent $500 on stock initially and sold it again right now, I'd have made $5.65.

That won't seem like a lot, but say I invest in a dozen stocks simultaneously and work for eight hours a day, five days a week. Some losses are, of course, more significant than others, and let's say 50% of your trader make a profit, and the rest lose. On this profit margin, I'd be making $271 per day, minus the fees from the broker.

That's $1,356 per five-day week, just making money on 12 stocks in that same time frame making the same profit, and only 50% of them are making profits.

Of course, the stock market is not that simple, and you may make a loss on every single trade one day and win small the next. You can't guarantee everything, but this should show you that making money is possible and how small wins add up to significant gains.

And that's it. As I said, this chapter is short and sweet and gets to the point, but hopefully, at this point, you've made your first investment and sale and can now officially call yourself a stock market investor. If you haven't, stop hanging around and go and do it! Take a moment to be proud of how far you've come and realize you've just taken your first big step on a lifelong journey.

With the core foundations laid, now it's time to get into the basics of stock market investment.

Chapter Four:

The Stock Market Basics

When you sign onto your broker website for the first time or looking into buyer any stock, what do you see? A load of line graphs, abbreviated terms, percentages in reds and greens here, there, and everywhere, and a ton of statistics which you have no idea what they mean. Don't worry; everyone starts here at some point.

This chapter aims to address these areas of concerns, giving you everything you need to know when it comes to mastering the basics of the stock market and having all the information you'll ever need to know in one handy chapter you can refer back to at any time.

Let's get into it.

Stocks and Shares

Stocks and shares are two different elements, both of which can be invested in individually. A stock is a certificate of ownership in a company. You're actually buying a percentage of a company, but don't get too excited. If you buy one share of a large company, the chances are this stock represents something like 0.00001% of the company, so you're not going to be making any big decisions any time soon.

Unsurprisingly, stocks are listed, bought, and sold on the stock market and can be purchased by anyone. Stock prices typically reflect the value of the company itself as a whole.

On the other hand, shares refer to the proportional ownership someone has in a company. For example, having 100,000 shares in a company of 2 million shares gives that person a 5% ownership of that company. They would be asked about things like company development and direction.

While you can buy and trade shares in a company, that's a whole other ball game with its own terminology and strategy. For the purposes of clarity, we're going to be sticking with stock trading.

Trading and Investing

There are two main ways to make money at the core of stock market investments. You can trade your stocks, which means buying them and selling them over a short period of time. This period usually lasts between a few minutes to an hour and is similar to the trading process we spoke about in the previous chapter. Small gains over time make big profits. You're making money off the tiny fluctuations in the daily stock market.,

On the other hand, investing is buying into a stock and then holding onto it for a longer period of time, a period that could last years or even decades. This is the way Warren Buffett has made his fortune. For example, when Netflix was starting up back in 1997, it was a tiny company. It went public back in 2002.

Using the Netflix investor calculator, if you had invested $500 into Netflix the day it went public, as of January 2021, your original investment, with no money added to it, would be worth $212,215. That's a profit of over 42,000%. Now, that's a tremendous amount of money, but you would have had to have taken the risk and invested all the way back in 2002, and then have the patience to wait 20 years to get to this sum without touching your money.

Worthwhile, yes, but Netflix is one company out of hundreds of thousands. If you invested in the wrong company, you would never have secured that amount of profit. This is, again, where the risk of stock market investment comes into play.

Whether you get involved in trading or investing is entirely up to you, and you may want to dabble in both, which is fine. It's all about getting educated, learning how to read the market, and then looking for opportunities when they arise.

The Language of the Stock Market

The words, phrases, and terms the stock market uses are enough to put anybody off, which is why I'm going to take the time to break everything down and show you what's what. Feel free to take this page and bookmark it as you may want to refer back to it at some point in the near future until you've committed the terms to memory.

Stock Market Term	Definition
Day Trading	The strategy of stock market trading where the trader will buy and sell stocks within the span of a single day. Sometimes called an active trader or day trader.
Dividend	A portion of earnings that a company will pay to shareholders or stock owners quarterly or annually.
An Exchange	This is where stocks and other different investments are traded throughout the world. Some of the most renowned exchanges in the US are places like the New York Stock Exchange and the Nasdaq.
An Index	Indexes are typically used as benchmarks for traders looking

Stock Market Term	Definition
	for a good deal. You may find a deal that gives a 10% return, which sounds pretty good, but if the market index shows that the average return is 13%, then 10% isn't actually that good, and something may be making this a bad investment. Some examples of popular indexes include places like the Dow Jones Industrial Index.
CFD	Stands for 'Contract for Differences.' Refers to the agreed price that an investor and CFD broker will trade a stock or other financial product for. It's basically security that you'll get paid the value that the stock is worth.
Open / Close	In the US, the stock market is open for trading at 9:30 am every day, which are the New York Stock Exchange and Nasdaq's operating times. Close is the closing time of the markets when no further trades can be made. In the US, this is 4 pm.
Portfolio	The collection of stocks that you, a trader, currently own at any one time. If you are presently in possession of five

Stock Market Term	Definition
	stocks, this collection of stocks is known as your 'portfolio.'
Spread	This term refers to the difference in value that a stock price asks for and any bids made on that stock, aka, the amount someone is willing to pay for it.

For example, if a stock is worth $20, but something is only willing to pay $18, the spread is $2. |
| Volume | Simply refers to the number of stocks that are being transferred. You may see a large volume of stocks being traded in one company. One thousand stocks is a much larger volume than ten stocks. |

There are more terms out there, but this table should cover the basics of what you need to know and what you'll come across as you go about your trades. Of course, once you come across new terms, you can start implementing them into your practices, but now, get to grips with and master the basics.

Once you're ready, let's move on to perhaps the most critical aspect of stock market trading, and that's choosing the stocks that are actually right for you and will hopefully make you money, thus generating the wealth you initially set out to create.

Chapter Five:

How to Choose the Right Stocks

For many readers out, this is perhaps the chapter you've been waiting for. There's no denying that the process of buying and selling stocks, referring to the actual practicality and physical motions of making a trade, is reasonably straightforward. What isn't easy is figuring out how to choose what stocks you're trading in the first place, which is not easy to answer since there's no right or wrong way to go about it.

There are just more favorable and less favorable ways of going about it. Within this chapter, I'm going to share with you the lowdown of how you can get educated in stocks, up to date with the markets, and make the best purchasing decisions possible.

Things to First Consider

When you buy a stock, what you're actually doing is purchasing a bit of ownership from a company and then repeating this process with various companies. These certificates of ownership come together to create your portfolio. You can think of this in a literal sense that you have a folder and a certificate for each stock you own, but nowadays, this is just your broker account, and everything is typically digital.

The first thing you want to start with is asking yourself what goals you want your portfolio to have and what direction you want to take it. Let's start with your goals. Of course, the primary goal number one is to make money. That's a given, but what kind of money are you trying to make? Are you making money so you can afford to have a vacation every year with it impacting your bank account?

Are you trying to make millions of dollars over the next decade? Are you saving up for a retirement fund? Whichever goal you want, you're going to approach creating your portfolio in a very different way, and therefore your strategies will change.

Suppose you're looking to make a lot of money. In that case, you're going to want to play the long game, which means making investments in small companies now that you hope are going to be significant in ten or twenty years, just like Netflix, potentially making hundreds of thousands of dollars on low investments.

Taking one of the most respected long-term investors, Warren Buffett, started when he was 14 years old with $5,000, and at the age of 83, he was worth $58.5 billion. He earned his first million at the age of 30. Warren is, without a doubt, absolutely loaded, but it took him 69 years to get there.

On the other hand, if you want to make $5,000 per year, so you can leave comfortably, you can get away with day trading and trying to aim for lots of little trading wins. Whatever your goal, this will determine your strategy and what stocks you'll buy, so get goal setting and have complete clarity with what you want to achieve!

Getting Educated

Now comes the enjoyable bit. The vast majority of your time as a stock trader will be spent on this point, and that's getting educated about the stock market, learning everything you need to know about your chosen industry, and just getting familiar with the stock market.

To start with, pick an industry you're interested in. You're going to be spending so much time reading up and following the news and trends of specific industries that you're going to begin to hate your life if you don't actually enjoy what you're interacting with nor find it interesting.

So, ask yourself, what are you interested in? Here are some industry ideas to get you started:

- Airlines

- Clothing and fashion

- Broadcasting networks and television

- Renewable energy

- Technology

- Environmental services

- Engineering and construction companies

- Hotels and holiday resorts

- Movies and entertainment

- Restaurant chains

- Wireless communication

There are literally hundreds of industries to get started in, so explore them all and take your pick. Let's say, just for simplicity, you love technology. You love having and reading about the latest tech and gadgets, so you want to start investing.

Now you need to start reading about the industry and the brands within. Some technology brands you may think about investing in, for example, could be;

- Apple

- Samsung

- Google

- Netflix

- Xerox

- Qualcomm Inc

Again, as an example, let's say you love phone technology and want to invest in Apple and Samsung technology. You then need to read up on these brands and find out what they're doing. What products are they working on? How do customers see and look at these brands? What kind of financial standing are these companies in? (More on this in the following sections).

Let's say you're reading the newspaper or technology blogs one morning, and Apple announces a brand-new mega iPhone is coming out in two years. Boom. You have yourself an investment opportunity because Apple stock is going to rise since other investors, some of which won't even be interested in technology, will buy into the stock while it's low, hoping to cash in when the mega iPhone comes to sale.

Even announcing news like this is going to make the stock go up because people get excited. This could also happen when Apple holds its annual summits to talk about all the new products they're working on and releasing over the coming years.

However, the next day you read the news, and it turns out older Apple models have been discovered to have faulty batteries causing overheating and safety issues. Now people are panicking that Apple is a lousy company the stock price is dropping.

Because you're following this information, you now have choices to make. Do you sell your stock because everyone else is and the company's value is dropping, or do you buy more stock because the public will get over the fault, and you'll make even more money on your investment when the mega iPhone comes out?

The choice is up to you, but the important point I'm trying to make is that you won't be able to make educated decisions unless you're keeping yourself updated with the latest news and trends.

Reading the news and latest updates are vital when it comes to finding new opportunities to invest. Even if not seemingly related, news in one industry can affect everything. Have nickel prices in the world dropped? Perhaps Apple can now make batteries more affordably and will create more stock, thus raising the value of the company? Have Samsung blundered their pre-orders for the latest devices, so now Android users will move over to Google phones instead of Samsung ones? There are obviously infinite possibilities for what could happen.

You just need to decide on what you think is most likely going to occur.

Just remember, knowledge is power.

Creating a Diverse Portfolio

Another short but sweet point now. If you invest $10,000 in one company, and this is all the money you have, you're doing the worst thing a stock investor can do by putting all your eggs in one basket. What happened if the stock loses money? Well, you lost money.

On the other hand, if you invest $1,000 in ten different companies, you're going to win on some investments and lose on others, meaning that you'll be able to make gains over time. Investing in multiple portfolios and creating what is known as a diverse portfolio is essential to the success of any stock trader.

Bear this point in mind when you're creating your portfolio and choosing what companies to work with. This is all to cover your losses, minimizing what you're losing, and then allowing you to focus on maximizing your profits.

In other words, don't just stick with one company or stock and fully invest in it. This is a sure-fire way to lose all your money eventually.

Researching the Story

No matter what information you're getting involved in, you're reading a story. You could be reading an article or blog post, a newspaper report, looking at a stock value chart, watching a movie, or even talking to another trader or 'expert.' Even when you're looking at the raw financial data for a company, you're reading a story, so you need to decide a few things like:

- Is the information you're receiving reliable?

- Is it trustworthy?

- What's the source?

- What is the information actually telling you?

- Is this information valuable enough to make a trading decision?

The problem these days is that a lot of information sources will cherry-pick their data. I could say, hey, look at this stock. It's going to make a 10% increase in value tomorrow morning. I guarantee it. This sounds amazing, but when the company's value is only $100, and the stocks are worth $0.01, you're wasting your time.

Instead, looking into the raw data of potential companies is usually a great place to start because it can't really be cooked. You just see a company for what it is. So, let's look at this in a little more detail.

You could look into the dividends of a company. Suppose a company is paying out stable dividends to its shareholders. In that case, this is typically a sign that a company's finances are healthy because they can afford to give lots back. If a company is holding back and giving out less and fewer dividends as the years go by (you can check this data by going into the financial records of the past, readily available since all companies on the stock market have their financial information publicly available), you'll know that a company could be struggling.

Are you reading the blog of an 'expert' trader who's trying to sell you a subscription to something or sells ad space on their website? Are they legitimately trying to help give you valuable information, or are they trying to clickbait you into giving them website traffic, and therefore making money on ad revenue? This is up to you to decide.

At the end of the day, whatever information you're using, you need to determine the source, the value that it has, the relevancy of the data, and then whether you can make a purchasing decision from it. Of course, not one piece of information will determine a decision, but this will be you collecting as much data as possible, building an overall picture of what is happening in the world, and then making your decisions from here.

Finding Suitable Companies

At this point, you're in your preferred industry, and you're looking at the lay of the land and what's going on. Now it's time to pick the companies you want to invest in. Sure, you may already have some companies in mind that made you want to start stock investing in the first place, and that's fine. However, to diversify your portfolio, you need several stocks ins several companies. So how do you find them?

There are three ways that stock traders will find the best companies to invest in and have a broad idea of what companies are on offer in any industry. These are as follows.

Using EFTs

ETFs is a term that stands for 'exchange-traded funds.' These funds follow certain industries and will allow you to see the performance of the said industry. Within the fund, you'll see a collection of various stocks and companies that make up that industry; thus, you'll be able to see what's performing well and what isn't.

You can easily find ETFs online by conducting a quick Google search for something like 'industry name ETF.' For example, searching 'technology ETF' gives results for ETFs like Vanguard Information Technology, iShares U.S Technology ETF, and Technology Select Sector SPDR Fund.

Within the Technology Select Sector Fund, you'll find a list of a load of technology companies listed on the stock market, including popular choices like Apple, Mastercard, PayPal, and Salesforce. These are all viable options for you to invest in and some other companies you may be interested in from the same industry.

If you like, you can even invest in the ETF itself, giving you access to a broad range of stocks from the company list that can potentially help you achieve profit.

Making Use of a Screener

A 'Screener' is a stock-based search engine that allows you to search for viable companies and stocks based on the search criteria and search filters you enable. Many screeners will enable you to filter results by name, industry, and financial sector. They can even offer different results with filtering options like market cap, dividend yield, and other metrics you may want to know.

You can easily find stock screeners online by simply searching 'stock screener' into your preferred search engine. A straightforward one to use can be found at www.tradingview.com/screener.

Researching the Market

The final way to find companies is basically based on the fact you'll find companies as you're doing your research. Reading an article or blog post on trending technology topics will simply introduce you to new and relevant companies that you'll be able to look into any time, and you can then figure out whether you want to invest in them or not.

Using the Raw Data

By now, you should have some kind of idea of what industry you want, what companies exist, and what type of portfolio you want to work on creating and putting together. Throughout this chapter, you've already witnessed me saying that you can use the raw company data to see whether you want to invest in a company, and this is a core process you'll want to go through with every company you invest in.

Since stock market companies and *publicly* traded, this means all their financial data is *publicly* accessible. However, looking at these stats and figures for the first time and trying to comprehend what it all means can be somewhat confusing, so this section is here to help.

First, finding the data.

Let's say you want to invest in Apple, just as an easy example. Head over to Google and type in 'Apple financial data.' The top result reads 'Apple – Investor Relations.' Click this link, and you'll be able to see all the up-to-date data of the company, including first-quarter results, the annual shareholder meeting notes, and you will have access to all company financial data from the years 2005 to 2020.

There are also dedicated websites, such as MacroTrends, that will list out all the company data in an easy-to-read table that makes finding what you're looking for incredibly easy, as well as making it easier to compare with other companies.

Let's explore some of the metrics you'll encounter and what they mean.

Metric	Definition
P/E Ratio	Stands for Price to Earnings ratio. This figure details how much profit was paid to each shareholder by showing how much profit they made per share. For example, if a company trades stock for $60, and the company earnings were $2 per share, the company traded at a P/E ratio of 30. 30 times the earnings. The lower the figure, the better the stock value is.
PEG Ratio	Stands for Price-to-Earnings Growth ratio. Companies obviously grow at different rates, which can make it hard to compare various stock values. A PEG ratio exists to give a clear indicator across the board as to how well a company is growing or not. For example, if a company has a P/E ratio of 50 and is expected to have an earnings growth of 20% over the next five years, the PEG ratio would be 10.
P/B Ratio	Stands for the Price-to-Book ratio. This is the value of a company and the net value of all its assets combined. This would be the company's value if it chose to shut down right

Metric	Definition
	now and then sold everything it owned for profit.
Debt Ratio	Commonly referred to as the debt-to-EBITDA ratio. EBITDA = earnings before interest, tax, depreciation, and amortization. This is a clear indicator of how financially healthy a company is regarding its debt. If a company has a super-high debt ratio, is this a company you're going to want to invest in?

These are not the only figures you can look into, but they're definitely a good start and metrics you're going to want to wrap your head around and get a good understanding of. Then you can get more onto more complex metrics. However, these are the only forms of raw data you'll want to look into once you have mastered the basics.

For example, you can look at the staffing of a company and look for changes happening here. Has the company you're interested in just hired one of the best marketing directors in the business from a competitor? The chances are they will deliver some new and exciting marketing ideas that could raise the company value tenfold, raising the potential that this is a stock to invest in.

While nothing is guaranteed, it's this kind of information and news you want to keep your eyes open for.

Be Aware and Focused

While writing this, a fascinating piece of news has just popped up on my newsfeed that I believe is worth mentioning within this chapter. As of January 2021, Elon Musk was officially hailed as being the world's richest man. An impressive feat surpassing the likes of Bill Gates and Jeff Bezos, and a guy with such wealth, of course, has a massive impact on the world, the stock market included.

However, in early 2021, Musk tweeted a simple Tweet saying, 'use Signal.' He referred to the relatively new Signal communication app, which works like WhatsApp and Messenger but has a heavy focus on being open source and being the most privacy-friendly messaging app out there where users won't have messages read or data collected. The app has been endorsed by Musk and other high-profile players like Edward Snowden.

However, stock market investors mixed up which Signal stock Musk meant, and instead of investing in the Signal app, they invested in a stock known as Signal Advance. This is a small component manufacturing business that trades over-the-counter stocks.

Advance Signal stocks rose 438% after the tweet, peaking at around $70.85 per share, which is a far cry from the $0.60 they closed at the day before. It was the highest price the stock ever had since it went public back in 2014.

That means in just one day, after one tweet, the stock of a company soared by 64,292%, which is just insane. Now, there were plenty of opportunities here for money to be made, but it just goes to show how many investors jump at everything they hear straight away while not taking the time to think about what's going on nor researching what they were doing.

For better or for worse, I think this definitely an interesting story to think about.

And with that, you should have enough information to accurately source, locate, and choose which stocks and companies you want to invest in. Sure, once you're learning about companies, getting an idea for what companies are stable and volatile, good and bad, getting started on the stock market can be slow. Still, once you're up to date and at a stage where you're just refreshing your knowledge with what is new and happening, you'll be breezing along in no time at all.

Chapter Six:

How to Create Wealth

As the title of this book suggests, the main aim of all the data here was for you to generate and create wealth in your life. Wealth is subjective. If you earn a million dollars a year, people will say you're rich, but if your expenses are a million dollars a year, then you're basically broke. If you only live on $30,000 a year but have a million in the bank, then you could live for 33 years without earning another penny. This is wealth.

It doesn't matter what attracted you to invest in stock in the first place. You cannot generate wealth if you're not developing your mindset to create wealth. In other words, if you're spending everything you earned straight away and you're not focused on how you're spending your money, then you're still going to be no better off than when you started invested, and you'll have nothing to show for your efforts.

This is why this chapter is dedicated to teaching you the basics, and some advanced aspects, of how you can adapt and improve your lifestyle to have money in the bank, to grow your wealth, and to take the stresses out of your own financial situation, regardless of what that may currently be.

Start Paying Attention to Your Finances

With individual and national debt seemingly spiraling out of control in many countries worldwide, so many people have fallen into the habit of ignoring their bank accounts. If you're in debt or continuously in your overdraft, then, of course, you don't want to keep looking at your account and reminding yourself every day, but this is something you're going to need to start doing.

If you're not at least focusing on your finances and thinking about what direction you want to take yourself, then you're never going to get anywhere. You need to start focusing. Every time you go to spend money or have the urge to make an impulse purchase, notice this impulse happening and ask yourself whether this is a purchase you want to make.

We'll talk about basic money management techniques later in the chapter, but for now, I just want you to focus on breaking any taboo or shame or guilt you may have about your finances and start focusing on them. Once you can accept where you are right now, you can begin taking steps to grow or remedy whatever situation you may be in.

Focus on Your Spending

What are you spending your money on, and where? Do you have gym memberships you're paying for but aren't using? Do you have a subscription to every streaming service and TV network provider service under the sun, but don't use them all, or at least don't need to use them all?

How much money are you spending on your car? Are you buying lots of fancy clothes to show off to people, or do they genuinely make you happy? Are you living in a house that's massive because it feels nice, or could you downgrade and save a ton of money in the meantime? Are you basically buying crap that you don't really want or need, but buy it just because you think it's cool?

We live in a world where you're conditioned through peer pressure and advertising to spend money on everything because, guess what, companies want to make money, and you are the person they can get it from. Start developing a mindset where you're mindful of what you're spending your money on and where and try to cut back where you can.

Try to make services and only spend money on what you want and need, and you'll instantly start seeing how much money you can accumulate just from doing this. Next time you order something from Amazon, do you really need to spend that $3 on next-day delivery, or can you get free delivery and wait an extra day or two? Of course, you can. Better yet, do you need to make that purchase, to begin with?

Think about it.

Start Saving

If there's money in your bank account, then the chances are you're going to want to spend it. When you start making money through stocks or side hustles, you will just end up spending the money because you know it's there. Ultimately, you'll never be better off than when you started, you'll just be spending more.

To counter this, it's a good idea to start saving your money in a dedicated savings account by putting a portion of what you earn in there every time you get paid. While experts differ, the average suggestion is to save between 30 and 50% of everything you make.

This means as soon as you get paid, you're sticking 50% of that pay packet straight into a savings account and leaving it there, then trying to live off the remaining 50%. This is another fantastic way you'll generate wealth without actually doing too much.

Think of it this way, if you're able to cut your expenses down, so you're able to save, let's say, 40% of your wage. You set up a direct debit and currently earn $1,500 per month through your full-time job. You save $400 as soon as you get paid and work to leave comfortably off the rest. With good stock market investment strategies, you're now earning around $2,000 a month.

Over the course of a year, your savings account has gone from $0 to a whopping $9600. How insane is that? In ten years, you've just saved $96,000, and that's sitting in your bank account, ready for you to use whenever or if ever you need it. Maybe you don't even need that much and choose to transfer $40,000 back into your current account to buy a house or go on vacation. It's up to you. It's your money.

Of course, 50% may be so high for some readers, which is understandable, so go through your finances and figure out what kind of percentage you can save, set yourself a target, and then aim always to put that amount of money into your savings account every single month. The more you save, the wealthier you'll be.

I know we've covered a lot in this chapter about making wealth, and while there are other techniques out there, this is an excellent foundation to start with. In doing so, you'll see such a dramatic shift in your personal financial situation. If you're stressed out about your finances and money situation, start with these points and see how much of a positive difference it can make.

Chapter Seven:
Investing in Real Estate and
Other High-Value Assets

Once you start making money and perhaps have a few thousand dollars sitting in your bank account, note your savings account should still have money in it that you're not going to touch, you might want to start thinking about moving away from trading on the stock market and moving onto more high-value assets. This basically means assets you can invest in and make more money than you would through stocks, aka. Real estate.

Now, even the mention of 'investing in real estate' may sound like some far-off dream that would never even know where to start, but trust me, it's not as difficult as you may think. Investing in real estate can be an incredibly lucrative and rewarding venture, but you do need the financing and wealth to make those initial purchases and investments.

By following the tips and strategies detailed in the book over the following years, this is an investment you should have. Thus, you can upgrade your investment efforts into property. This means you'll be able to make more money, more quickly, therefore increasing the rate at which you can generate your wealth. Sounds good, right?

Throughout this chapter, I'm going to detail exactly how you can get started in real estate investment, what you need to look out for and get educated in, and how you can start earning money through the property ladder and investing in the right places at the right time.

Making Money in Real Estate:
The Rundown

First of all, I want to take a moment to explain how money is actually made in real estate so that we're on the same page and you know how it all works. Fortunately, there are multiple ways in which it works. I'll go into some more detail for some of these later on in the chapter, but for now, here's the rundown of how real estate investment works.

One popular way to make money is by flipping a house. This is to buy a property while it's cheap, invest some money into it to make it better condition than when you first purchased it, and then sell it for more money. This is a great way to make money as you could buy a somewhat rundown house for $50,000. You may then spend another $50,000 doing the property up, and then you can sell it for $150,000. You've just made $50,000.

There are both pros and cons to this approach, namely that you risk buying a property that you can't sell, or you may purchase a property with a ton of problems you didn't foresee. Now you're spending way more money on renovations that are eating into your profit margins and so on, but when the going goes well, this is a very lucrative approach to make.

The second approach you can take is flipping a property over time. This is the act of merely buying a property and then holding onto it for some time. Typically, the value of a property will increase over time as the area develops. When a house becomes better connected, has access to better facilities like schools, shops, and entertainment, and is in a nicer area, all these factors will increase a property's value.

Of course, there are exceptions. If you purchase a property in the middle of nowhere that is high value and coveted for its privacy, this can be ideal in the right markets. However, you're not going to find somewhere like this on a $50,000 deposit.

The final and perhaps most lucrative way to make money consistently is buying properties to let. This, as the name suggests, means buying any kind of property, from an apartment to a house, and then renting it out for a monthly fee. This could be both commercial or residential property, and if you're charging monthly, it can give you a good profit every month.

The great thing about buying property is that you can take a mortgage and make repayments every month without paying the house's full amount upfront. This means higher value properties are within your reach, even if you don't have the total sum. Using average mortgage rates and prices, this is what the maths would look like.

Making Money in
Real Estate via a Rental:
(A Case Study)

You buy a home that costs $350,000 in a friendly, developed area that doesn't have any problems. Just a typical family home. You put down a down payment (deposit) for around 14-15%, meaning you're taking out a mortgage for $300,000 and have a deposit of $50,000. Chuck in an interest rate of 3%, without other fees, you're going to be looking at mortgage repayments of around $1,500 per month for the next 29 years.

Now, the price you can rent a house out for will vary dramatically depending on the location and a ton of other variables, but looking at somewhere like somewhere mid-range, like Newton, Massachusetts, you're looking at payable rent of around $2,300 per month.

So, to summarize, you're saving up and paying $50,000 for a deposit on a house (remembering that deposits are variable and can change to suit your personal financial situation) and purchasing a $350,000 home.

Paying back $1,500 per month but gaining $2,300 per month in rent, you're making $800 a month in profit. That's for just owning a house and leasing it out to someone else. You can either save this money and pay your mortgage off quicker, so you're then earning $2,300 per month in profit or live off the money.

If you save $600 per month of this profit, you'll have another $50,000 deposit to buy another house in just under seven years. Over the course of 50 years of your life, just with one house using these examples, you'll have around $80,000 in the bank, and you'll own a $350,000 home.

Now, don't start thinking this is plain sailing because it's not. Let's dive into the ins and outs of real estate property rental investments so you can get a clear idea of what you're working with.

Rental Property Investment Explained

While owning rental properties is a great way to earn money, especially if you own multiple properties, there are pros and cons to getting involved, just like there is in stock market investment.

Firstly, you need to find the right property. This means taking time to find the right house in the right area for just the right price, and this is no easy task. In fact, it's really rather tricky. You don't just commit and buy the first house you come across, but we'll speak more about this later in the chapter.

You could end up buying a lovely, ready-to-rent house, but this is going to cost a lot of money to begin with, potentially because someone else is already selling it as an investment. On the other hand, you could buy a rundown property that needs renovation, perhaps a property on auction. While you might get it at a great steal of a price, you'll need to invest money in making sure the property is in an acceptable condition to rent, and someone is actually going to want to live in it.

Like choosing stocks, this requires patience and looking for the right opportunity to come along at the right time, and spending time researching the property market and seeing what people are looking for what properties, but indeed your skills from stock market investment and getting educated will help with this process dramatically.

Now come the real variables that can make and break your success.

Perhaps the biggest con of rental properties is finding tenants to put into your house or residence. If you're working with commercial properties, then you need to find businesses to let what you're offering.

Most tenants, in most cases, will probably be okay. They'll sign the contract and move in, and everything will be okay. However, of course, you've got to find these tenants in the first place, and there's no guarantee they're going to be saint-like. I'm sure you've heard of the horror stories some landlords will speak of about how people have moved in and trashed the place, costing a ton of damage to fix.

Of course, this isn't going to happen with every tenant and only stands out as a horror story because it's an extreme case, but that doesn't mean it's impossible and not going to happen. It is possible. You could use the help of a letting agent who can find, let, vet, and manage your tenants on your behalf, which might be a good idea once you have multiple properties, but this will eat terribly into your profit.

However, on the other side of the coin, renting a property does provide significant monthly income that's regular and goes straight into your pocket. It maximizes the value of any capital and savings you might be holding on to. Why have $50,000 sitting in a savings account earning 1 or 2% interest per year when you could be making $800 per month profit through real estate investment?

What's more, lots of people flock to real estate investment because there are a few benefits you won't get elsewhere, such as tax-deductible expenses, but this will solely depend on where you are in the world and the rules and regulations surrounding this at the time.

Property Flipping Investment Explained

If you don't want to get involved with property rental and it seems like too much trouble, then perhaps property flipping is right for you. As I said above, this is basically the process of buying a house that looks as though he needs some work for an affordable price, doing the necessary renovations and upgrade work, and then selling the property for more than you bought it for.

You then take the capital you make on the property, buy another property, and keep repeating the process. Sounds nice and simple. Let's look at the math. Of course, the math can vary dramatically depending on how much you buy the house for, what work needs to be done, what hidden costs there are, and how much you're able to sell the house for at the end.

If you buy a house, do it up, and then there's a COVID-19 pandemic or economic crash, selling the home could be a lot harder than the time in which you bought it, so these are risks you need to consider. Anyway, to the math.

Conducting a quick online search, you can buy a reasonably decent, three-bedroom house in a nice area for around $180,000. Suppose you go to auction, perhaps buying seized properties from the US Department Treasury, which I highly recommend looking at for inspiration of what's available. In that case, the prices can vary wildly. Some days you may find some fantastic deals because no one else is interested, and some days people will pay way more than you would ever expect anyone to pay. That's just how it goes.

So, let's say you buy a property with all essential services connected and no real major problems for $180,000. You buy it on a mortgage or loan with an extra $40,000 to kit it out. You end up spending $35,000 and sell the property on the market a few months later for $280,000. After paying back the mortgage, you've just made between $50,000 and $80,000 over the course of a few months, which are profits not to be sniffed at.

Again, there are a ton of variables that can affect the price, such as whether you're going to get tradespeople in to do the work (eating into your profit) or you're going to do the work yourself, which could save you a ton of money, but it's going to eat a lot of your time.

This is the thing with property flipping. Most people will see this as a long-term investment strategy because you're only really going to be able to focus on one, maybe two properties at once, and these could take a year or more to complete. Still, $160,000 a year for two properties is not bad money at all.

How to Choose the
Right Property to Invest In

Perhaps the fundamental question you're going to be asking yourself when getting involved with real estate investment, especially when you're just starting out, is what kind of property are you looking for? Which type of property is actually going to be worthwhile?

Unfortunately, there's no right or wrong answer. The market is continuously shifting and changing all the time, and you never know who is out there looking for a new property nor what they're interested in. You have to basically get your property to the best possible state and then hope for the best.

However, that being said, there are endless ways you increase your chances of finding a tenant or securing a sale, and that's by considering the criteria below before making a purchase or developmental investment.

Defining Your Ideal Buyer

You can't sell to everyone because everyone is looking for different things when buying a house. As a seller or landlord, you need to narrow down the kind of buyer you want interested in your property, which will help you endlessly with the rest of the criteria below. Let me give you some target buyer examples.

- A student looking to attend a nearby university

- A family with two children and a dog

- A bachelor working in the city

- A house for newlyweds

- A house for a retired couple

- A property for someone looking for temporary accommodation

As you can see, as you read each example of this list, you have a clear idea of what kind of criteria you'll be working towards when working on a property. Students will be looking for traditional, affordable, and bare essential ways of living but want a good location.

A family will be looking for access to schools and amenities but will want an affordable price, possibly a garden, and a child-friendly area. The more specific you can be in defining your ideal buyer, the easier it will be to sell your property because you'll know exactly who you're focusing on.

Budget

Usually, the main concern for anyone looking to buy a property is to fit your target audience's budget. There's no point getting a three-bedroom family home and getting it out to the teeth, so it's then worth over a million. No family in a typical suburban area will buy it because they simply can't afford it.

Wherever your location is, and no matter what kind of house you have, you need to make sure it will be within the budget range of someone most likely to buy it. When you're pricing your properties and calculating how much profit you can make on an investment, look for other similar properties in the area that match the quality of what you'll be offering for an idea of how much you can get back and how much profit you'll be making.

The Size

When it comes to property, for many people, size does matter. If a buyer is going to spend a lot of money to live in an upmarket New York apartment, then they're not going to want some kind of cramped shoebox like flat, but a lovely spacious apartment with open views. However, size does cost, so you need to think of your ideal buyer and whom you're marketing to.

Location

Location is perhaps the most crucial aspect when it comes to choosing a property because it determines everything from the kind of buyer who will be interested in the price of the property itself—living next to an airport? You're probably going to have a lower price because of the noise and air traffic.

Found a small apartment that's ideal for a flight attendant working at the airlines who will be working away most of the time? This could be a perfect investment opportunity.

Student housing and renting is widespread in most major cities and a great example of why location matters. If you're in the city center and there are lots of bars, access to transport and shops, and the university itself, then you can charge a lot of money on a months' rent because your property is in such a prime location. However, with such an expensive price tag, you're drastically limiting the number of students who will be able to consider your property because students typically live on a small budget.

If you have a property on the city center limits, you can make the property more affordable because it's not in such a prime location, so while you're earning less money, you'll be much more likely to find a buyer who can afford and keep up with payments.

It's all about finding the right balance for the right price for the right person.

Explore the Area

While property location matters, the property location's location also matters, sometimes even more than the property itself. Found a gorgeous house, but criminal gangs run the surrounding area? You're probably not going to get a family moving in any time soon.

Got a studio apartment perfect for someone wanting to live and work in the big city, but there's a huge high-paying, blue-chip job slump right now? Probably not the best investment. If you know the location you're buying in, such as your home city, then great, you probably know where you're living quite well.

However, if you're buying in a new city or town that you haven't lived in and don't know anything about, then make sure you're doing your research and seeing whether your ideal buyer or tenant is actually going to want to live in a place like this. Some things to consider include:

- Shops

- Entertainment

- Schools

- Environment

- Crime rates

- Recent events and news

- Neighboring area

- Government or council laws and regulations

- Political lenience

And so on. Take some time to research before leaping into an investment because you don't want to get caught out.

Get a Property Inspection

The chances are you've heard the horror stories of investors who have bought houses at auction and similar places, had massive dreams to turn into a wonderful place, only to find there was a whole list of hidden problems that are going to cost an absolute fortune to fix and will leave you with no profit whatsoever.

There's no doubt that any kind of large scale and complicated project will have setbacks and unforeseen problems that will take you over budget, but so many of them can be avoided by inspecting the property in the first place. Sure, inspections can be expensive, but it's far cheaper than just buying a property and having to spend half as much again trying to get it to a liveable standard.

In some cases, many properties may be being sold with inspections already completed, which is great, but make sure you're taking these with a pinch of salt. Some homeowners may have friends who carry out checks or just say they had had one when they didn't, so always ask for proof. You don't want to be spending hundreds of thousands of dollars on what is essentially a faulty product you can't get a refund for.

Of course, I could go on all day and could write an entire book on how property development and real estate investment can make you money. Still, for now, you should now know all the basics and the foundations you need to know to see why it's an investment strategy worth thinking about, especially as your starting capital begins to grow over the next coming years.

Chapter Eight:
Moving to the Future

As we draw to the end of this book, you should have everything you need to know when it comes to grasping the basics, setting a core foundation, and learning everything there is to know when it comes to getting involved with the art of investing. Whether you're looking into stock market investment, real estate, building your wealth, or even just developing your own personal money management skills, we've covered it all, and now you can easily put your best foot forward.

So, what does the future look like?

Well, as with anything you start doing in life for the first time, it's going to take some time and some getting used to when grasping the basics and getting used to everything. However, the more you do something and the more experience you have, the better off you'll be, the more practiced you'll become, and the more experience you'll have.

This creates a snowball effect where you'll keep learning and continue to get better, further enhancing your skills more and more, honing your craft, and becoming more confident in your own abilities. Nobody was born a true investor with an understanding of what to do and where to start. All the greats and everyone who has ever tried has been through the stage you're at right now.

This means you need to have a dab of perseverance and determination to keep going. There are going to be rough and tough times when things don't pan out the way you expected them to, and you're making losses that are making you feel down, out, and as though you want to give everything up. These are the times you need to keep going.

That's not saying you should commit to your strategy and just keep going until you burn out or run out of money. That's foolish. Of course, you need to learn when to cut your losses, but giving up on your dream is the only true way you'll ever going to fail. That's a guaranteed loss.

As with any aspect of life, when you go through a hard time, take a moment to reflect on what's going on, to evaluate what's going on to the best of your ability, and to learn any lessons that can be learned along the way. This is how you'll get better and how you'll be able to improve and be the best you can be.

I use Warren Buffett as an example because he's one of the most revered investors in the world and good at what he does, but even someone who's in such a successful position as he didn't get to where he is today just by winning. He's made huge losses during his time and didn't always live such a glamourous lifestyle.

Due to travel restrictions implemented during the COVID-19 pandemic, the travel and airline industry has taken a tremendous hit, and Warren's own Berkshire Hathaway company is said to have lost a massive $70 billion off its market value. Imagine having to deal with those kinds of losses but still being able to take a deep breath, put your head on straight, and continue to make decisions to the best of your ability.

Developing this kind of attitude towards life doesn't come overnight but is developed and nurtured through years of experience, trial and error, and by having a can-do attitude. Start working towards it now, and you'll see great things come from it in your future.

Final Thoughts & Conclusion

And with that, we reach the end of the line, and now it's all over to you! At this point, you should really know everything there is to know when it comes to getting off the ground with stock market investment, and hopefully, you've already been working along with this book and are starting to make some money.

Remember, patience is the key to success, coupled with dedication and open-mindedness. You're not going to get everything right the first time since you're only a human being, but being able to stay grounded and present will help you learn from your mistakes. There is no limit or skill cap to what you can achieve.

Whatever kind of investment strategy you go opt for, no matter what your portfolio goals are or where your investment journey takes you, whether, into real estate markets or your own comfortable financial situation, I wish you the best of luck.

That's it from me, but before I go, I just want to give a quick shoutout to everyone who made this book possible. You know who you are.

I also want to ask quickly that if you enjoyed the book or want to give me some feedback, I would love to hear what you've got to say. Simply drop a review wherever you picked up your copy and let me know your thoughts. I love reading any and all comments, and I find them incredibly inspiring. Just like all humans, I want to get better at my craft and become the best I can be, so if there are any improvements to make, let me know!

I look forward to hearing from you and wish you all the best on your journey! I hope to see you soon!

Disclaimer

This book contains opinions and ideas of the author and is meant to teach the reader informative and helpful knowledge while due care should be taken by the user in the application of the information provided. The instructions and strategies are possibly not right for every reader and there is no guarantee that they work for everyone. Using this book and implementing the information/recipes therein contained is explicitly your own responsibility and risk. This work with all its contents, does not guarantee correctness, completion, quality or correctness of the provided information. Misinformation or misprints cannot be completely eliminated.

Printed in Great Britain
by Amazon